BIG SOUTH FORK COUNTRY

BIG
SOUTH
FORK
COUNTRY

Photography by
SENATOR
HOWARD BAKER
and
JOHN NETHERTON

Text by Howard Baker

ACKNOWLEDGMENTS

Tom DeJean, Anne Malanka, David Badger, Steve Bakaletz,
Bill Dickinson, J. T. Baker, Jim Reed, Kennedy Reed,
Dr. Frank Thomas, Pat Thomas, Steve Seven, Neil Sexton,
Fred Marcum, Pat Butler, Bob Wheely, Jack Laxton,
Ronnie Lloyd.

Published in Nashville, Tennessee, by Rutledge Hill Press,
211 Seventh Avenue North, Nashville, Tennessee 37219

Book design and typography by Bruce Gore/Gore Studio, Inc.,
Nashville, Tennessee

Engraving by Capitol Engraving Co., Nashville, Tennessee

Printed and bound by Horowitz/Rae Book Manufacturers, Fairfield,
New Jersey.

Library of Congress Cataloging-in-Publication Data

Baker, Howard H. (Howard Henry), 1925–
    Big South Fork country / photography by Howard Baker and
John Netherton; text by Howard Baker.
      p.   cm.
    ISBN 1-55853-258-7
    1. Big South Fork National River and Recreation Area (Tenn.
and Ky.)—Pictorial works. I. Netherton, John. II. Title.
F442.2.B34 1993
976.8'71—dc20   93-28260
                                                  CIP

Printed in the United States of America
1 2 3 4 5 6 7 8 — 98 97 96 95 94 93

MOUNTAIN people have many virtues, but one of the most attractive is their ability to verbalize both ordinary and extraordinary experiences. That is why, in addition to viewing pictures of the Big South Fork area in this book, you will meet some of the people who live here.

I have always thought there was much of the frontier spirit in the mountain idiom. Neil Sexton certainly has that. His matter-of-fact presentation of the story of the New River light contains an almost supernatural component.

Dr. Frank Thomas reflects the best qualities of the educated and professional people of the region. Men and women like him have led the cultural, civic, commercial, and industrial life of the area, but with a generous sense and pride of place.

While Big South Fork country is sparsely populated, many lose sight of the fact that some of the earliest pioneers who worked their way through the Cumberland Gap and westward before and just after the American Revolution took up residence on this rocky soil. Kennedy Reed's recitation of his family's participation in every war since the Revolution (except the Spanish-American War, which he claims wasn't much of a war anyway) says something about the volunteer spirit from which Tennessee takes its nickname.

Jack Laxton is an archetypical "high sheriff." My grandmother, who was also a sheriff, told me when I was seeking the Republican presidential nomination that I was making a mistake. She said that if I wanted to get close to power, I should run for sheriff instead. Both her attitude and Sheriff Laxton's service say something about the respect mountain people have for orderliness, law, and order.

My cousin J. T. Baker may be one of the few real geniuses I have ever met, not because he has a graduate degree in anything, but because he has a keen understanding and a wry appreciation of the realities of life. Sometimes his knowledge of esoterica amazes me; at other times I can hardly wait for him to shut up.

The stories presented here have no common thread except they are the product of this place and this time, and they fit my image of what the twentieth century pioneer is like. I hope you enjoy these vignettes. They are an important part of this portrait of Big South Fork country.

Howard Baker

To Joy

for her long understanding and tolerance
of my photographic foibles

—HOWARD BAKER

BIG SOUTH FORK COUNTRY

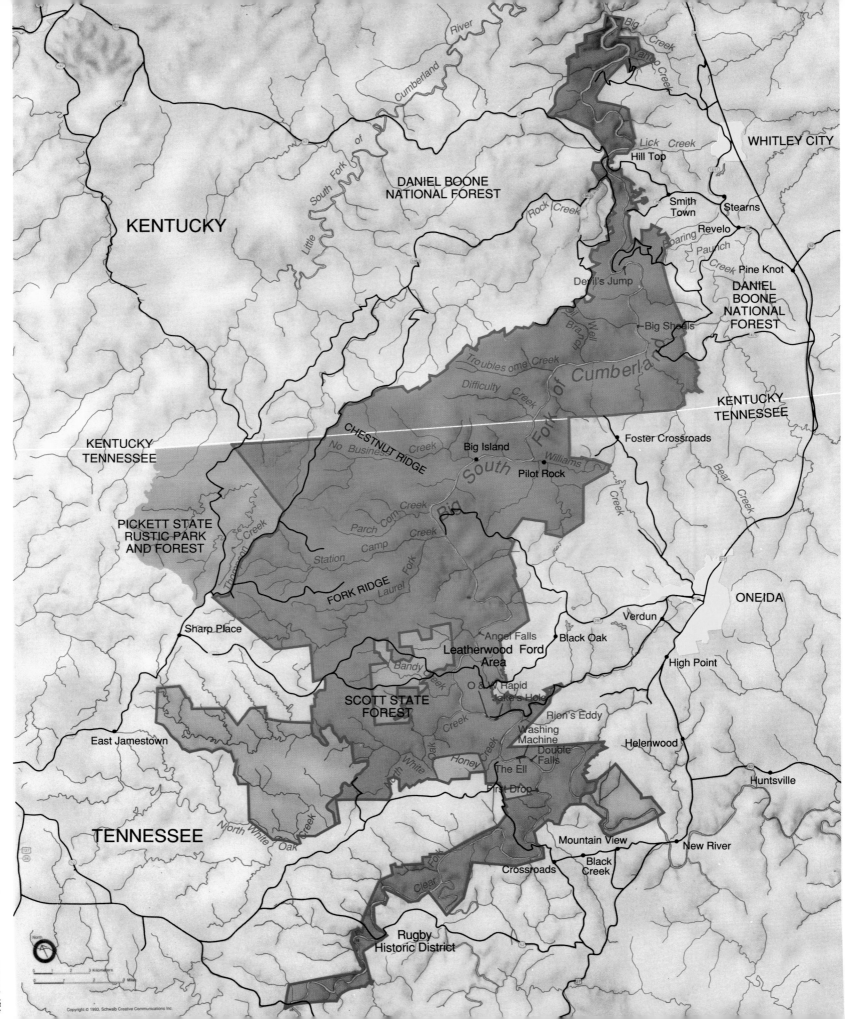

WHITLEY CITY

DANIEL BOONE
NATIONAL FOREST

KENTUCKY

Hill Top

Smith
Town   Stearns

Revelo

Pine Knot

DANIEL
BOONE
NATIONAL
FOREST

Devil's Jump

Big Shoals

Troublesome Creek

KENTUCKY
TENNESSEE

Difficulty

Creek

KENTUCKY
TENNESSEE

CHESTNUT RIDGE

Big Island

Foster Crossroads

Williams

Pilot Rock

PICKETT STATE
RUSTIC PARK
AND FOREST

Corn Creek

Parch   Camp

Station

FORK RIDGE

Laurel

Sharp Place

Angel Falls   Black Oak

Leatherwood Ford
Area

Verdun

High Point

Bandy

SCOTT STATE
FOREST

O & W Rapid
Jake's Hole

Rion's Eddy

Washing
Machine

Helenwood

East Jamestown

Honey Creek

Double
Falls

The Ell

First Drop

Huntsville

North White Oak

Creek

TENNESSEE

Mountain View

New River

Black
Creek

Crossroads

Clear

Rugby
Historic District

BIG SOUTH FORK
The Hidden Treasure of the Cumberlands

Howard H. Baker, Jr.

THE CUMBERLANDS were the first mountains John Muir ever saw, and it was in Tennessee in 1867 that the future founder of the Sierra Club first committed himself to conservation. His more famous travels through California's Sierra Madres were, so far as we Tennesseans are concerned, something of an afterthought. One look at the new Big South Fork National River and Recreation Area and it's easy to see why.

Around the Big South Fork, straddling the Kentucky-Tennessee border on the Cumberland Plateau, the modern visitor will come in contact with a ghostly community of coal miners, a Victorian social reformer who brought a patch of England to Tennessee, the most stunning natural architecture east of the Mississippi, thousands of prehistoric Indians (and their primordial barbeque pits), hundreds of species of unusual plants and animals, a river that appears to flow upstream, and a crayfish that hasn't changed a bit in 180 million years.

That crayfish could be the official mascot for the people who live in the Big South Fork region, because change is not high on our list of priorities, either:

■ On the Tennessee side of the border, we have elected a Republican (including my father and stepmother) to Congress every two years since 1858 until we fell victim to redistricting.

■ The Slavens, descendants of one of the area's first families, finally decided to bring electricity and running water into their home about twelve years ago.

■ And my cousin James Toomey Baker spoke for many when he proposed that our hometown of Huntsville, Tennessee, choose as its centennial theme A Century of Status Quo.

▲ *Expansive open fields dwarf the Bandy Creek Visitor Center, where tourists can talk with park naturalists.*

◄◄ *Map of the Big South Fork National River and Recreation Area.*

▲ *After heavy rains, fungi litter the park's landscape. There are more than
1,500 species of fungi in the Big South Fork area.*

No wonder John Muir liked it here so much. Here is conservatism at its most profound, but it's a personal rather than an ideological conservatism, the kind that springs from a genuine celebration of the world as it is, the kind that keeps people close to the earth and rejoices in life's simplest pleasures.

It's a conservatism less fired by political passion than warmed by a coal stove, but it's a rugged, protective philosophy all the same. A giant wooden slingshot in somebody's front yard guards an approach road to the Big South Fork, and it's the closest thing to symbolism we have in these parts.

These good, strong, friendly people (Sergeant Alvin York of World War I fame lived around here) are the perfect

▲ *Raccoons can be found around the Bandy Creek Campground almost any night as they pilfer food.*

hosts and stewards for one of the great hidden treasures of the natural world.

Because the Big South Fork is a new federal reserve, only 800,000 visitors came to see us in 1992, compared with 8 million who journeyed to the Great Smokies two hours south of here. We think we can accommodate a few more than 800,000, but frankly we don't want 8 million people a year tramping around in our mountains. We're going to share the secret of the Cumberlands with you, but we would prefer you didn't mention it to anyone else.

▲ *Mannequins dressed as coal miners are part of the Mine 18 exhibit at Blue Heron in the northern section of Big South Fork.*

◀ *The weathering of sandstone produced this odd-shaped rock shelter named Nee High.*

THE RIVER

For being a mere fork of a river, the Big South Fork is . . . well . . . big. It drains an area of 1,382 square miles in Tennessee's Scott, Fentress, Pickett, and Morgan counties, and in Kentucky's Wayne and McCreary counties. And it threads through 106,000 acres of federally protected recreation area, giving the river traveler a true sense of wilderness.

Rent a canoe or raft from the Cumberland Rapid Transit Company, and you can take the longest water ride in the eastern United States: six days to travel eighty miles of the Big South Fork National River. You will navigate a clear, free-flowing stream punctuated by rapids that range from mild to wild.

It is an ancient river, cutting through gorges more than 250 million years old; and it is one of only three rivers in the United States designated by Congress as a "national river," distinguished by its historical significance as well as its wild and scenic beauty.

The Big South Fork is also one of the few rivers in the eastern United States that hasn't been dammed for hydroelectric power generation or flood control, though not for lack of trying. The U.S. Army Corps of Engineers first proposed to dam the river in 1933 and construction was authorized several times in the 1950s and 1960s by the U.S. Senate, but the House of Representatives would never go along.

Rafters, canoers, and kayakers of every skill level—from novice to death-defying expert—can find a stretch of the Big South Fork that offers them relaxation and challenge. The river's rapids range in difficulty all the way from Class I (which even I can negotiate) to Class V (for people who like to swim in washing machines).

Many whitewater rafters training for the Colorado River rapids in the Grand Canyon come here first for a three-day "test drive." Between Burnt Mill Bridge and Leatherwood Ford (about an eleven-mile stretch of river) there are eight Class III and IV big water rapids, the mere thought of which I find exhausting.

In rapid succession, the rafter encounters First Drop, Double Falls, the Washing Machine, the Ell, Ryan's Eddy, the Narrows, Jake's Hole, and the Rapid at the O&W Bridge.

Things calm down for a while then, but just when you think you've mastered the river, you come upon the really difficult rapids. First, there's Angel Falls, a rapid made intentionally more dangerous with a blast of dynamite at the request of river paddlers about thirty years ago.

And then, a few miles farther downstream (which means north, remember), there's Devil's Jump, which is every bit as breathtaking as it sounds.

Wedged between sandstone walls 500 feet high, Devil's Jump was once the place where young boys—"rafting devils"—would jump aboard giant logs felled by lumberjacks and ride them on the Cumberland and Tennessee rivers all the way to the sawmills in Nashville. These treacherous journeys took two months; the boys would return home young men. At Devil's Jump today, the loggers are long gone, and the modern rafter shoots the Class III and IV rapids in the solitude of the wilderness.

Respectful as one must be of the awesome natural power of a river, it is reassuring to note that there has never been a fatality or a serious injury here under the supervision of any of the rafting companies operating on the river.

Long stretches of the river are safe enough for me to take my grandsons out in canoes. The main channel of the Big South Fork falls only about four feet per mile, a gentle slope as these things are measured.

I am reliably advised that for the fisherman (which I am not) the Big South Fork offers eight varieties of bass, eleven kinds of shiners, and such other delicacies as yellow bullhead, slender madtom, southern redbelly dace, shovelnose sturgeon, longear sunfish, and the ever-popular quillback carpsucker.

All of this is on a river that practically nobody knows about. Fifty people on the Big South Fork at the same time are a big crowd, and the river carries no more than three or four thousand people on its currents in a whole year.

Boating is best between the second week in March and the first of June, and there's a great half-day canoe trip from Pine Creek to Leatherwood Ford that's good until the end of July. But it's best not to make any whitewater rafting plans past June 1, as the water supply gets iffy after that.

THE LAND

You are not likely to find more spectacular scenery anywhere east of the Rockies than you will find in the Big South Fork. Imagine standing at the top of the Empire State Building and looking down at the streets of midtown Manhattan and you have some sense of the perspective one gets looking down from the Cumberland cliffs into the Big South Fork river valley hundreds of feet below. You have the feeling of standing on top of the world, and there is nothing like it.

Daniel Boone came here nearly two hundred years ago, and the land is still as he saw it: a wilderness undisturbed by civilization. Coming here at the end of the twentieth

▲ *Mist rises from a low river during a dry period.*

century, and, even with 150 million Americans within a day's drive of the place (8 million of them in the souvenir shops of Gatlinburg two hours away), your only conspicuous company is apt to be a blue heron soaring silently above you.

What you and the heron and Daniel Boone would see are massive sandstone bluffs carved in semicircles, white and scarlet oaks, tulip poplars, sugar maple, umbrella and cucumber magnolias, white ash, willows, sycamore, sweet gum, river birch, and hickory trees. You'll see dogwood, holly, sassafras, the spreading branches of hemlocks, the smooth bark of the gray beech, and a brilliant profusion of rhododendron, mountain laurel, and azalea.

You may also see white-tailed deer, wild hogs (descendants of Russian stock imported for the now-defunct Parch Corn Creek Hunting Lodge), southern flying squirrels, red and gray foxes, chipmunks, beaver, muskrat, mink, otter, painted turtles, bobcats, coyotes, long-tailed weasels, New England cottontails, hoary bats, silver-haired myotis, and eastern spotted skunks.

Birds—132 catalogued varieties of them—are seen everywhere, including the ruffed grouse (which sounds like a low-flying jet), the hairy and the pileated woodpecker, the screech owl, the red-tailed hawk, the scarlet tanager, the crow, the whippoorwill, the cardinal, the mockingbird, the turkey, and the last thing a turkey wants to see, the turkey vulture.

What you are less likely to see are things like the crayfish that lives in the streams around Roaring Paunch Creek. This is the crayfish whose 180-million-year-old ancestor lived in these parts before the Ice Age. The area around the Big South Fork is teeming with such biological wonders. No comprehensive biological census has been completed because when taxonomists come here to catalog the species, they always seem to find something new and decide the census can wait while they explore their discovery further.

What no wanderer in the Cumberland wilderness can miss are the extraordinary stone formations sculpted by the violent collision of continents and by the patient insistence of water flowing over—and, after million of years, through—solid rock.

It was the slamming together of the African and North American continents that formed the Cumberland Plateau itself 250 million years ago. But the more subtle formations—the cliffs, the natural arches, the rockhouses—were products of water wearing down sandstone. These grand and plentiful natural sculptures have led geologists to call the Big South Fork area "the Mesa Verde of the East."

Thousands of rockshelters and scores of natural arches are in the area, but the most spectacular are the Twin Arches, one of the largest natural bridges in the world. The larger South Arch has a clearance of 70 feet and a span of more than 135 feet. The North Arch has a 51-foot clearance and a 93-foot span. Once accessible only by a four-wheel-drive vehicle and a steep climb, the Twin Arches are now more visitor friendly with an approach road suitable for passenger cars and stairs leading to the arches themselves.

THE PEOPLE

Human history in the Big South Fork area began about 12,000 years ago with nomadic tribes of hunters who followed the elk, bison, deer, bear, and other large game animals to what is now Tennessee and Kentucky. The rockshelters that nature created were used as homesteads by these hunters, and 4,000 of these shelters—some amazingly well preserved by favorable elements—can be found within the Big South Fork Recreation Area. In all, there are 8,000 archaeological sites in the area, according to the National Park Service. (The Park Service also estimates that at one time there was one moonshine still for every 116 acres of the Big South Fork.)

There is evidence at these ancient sites of tremendous

human activity between 12,000 and 7,000 years ago. There is even evidence of prehistoric "clambakes," (actually, musselbakes) and of intentional burning of forests to clear land for primitive planting.

In the Bell Farm area in 1962, a Native American thousands of years old was found buried in a bearskin robe, skin and hair still intact, preserved by the dry air of a rockshelter that had served as a kind of time capsule.

The Bell Farm Indian is now safely preserved at the University of Kentucky, and scientists say it is possible the time capsule effect could yield similar archaeological treasures from other rockshelters in the area. The rockshelters, most of which have been severely looted, are now under the protection of the National Park Service and the Archaeological Resources Protection Act of 1979.

Evidence indicates that beginning 7,000 years ago, and for the next twenty centuries, human life in the Big South Fork area virtually vanished. Scientists speculate that a dramatic environmental change occurred during that time, most likely an elevation in temperature that diminished the water supply and drove the large game animals—and their hunters—off the plateau.

When they returned, after two millennia, the people of the Big South Fork were hunting smaller game, collecting plants, living in primitive campsites, and moving with the seasons. Between A.D. 900 and 1000 these people left the plateau for good and founded agricultural communities along the Tennessee and Cumberland rivers. Occasional hunting forays into the mountains were all that linked people with the Big South Fork for the next thousand years.

Long hunters changed all that when they first came to the area in the late 1700s. By 1800 several permanent homesteads had been established, but the fact that life was as hard for these settlers as for their prehistoric predecessors is obvious from their choice of such place-names as Difficulty, Troublesome, and No Business.

Even today, life isn't that easy. The farmers around here, for example, do not drive giant combines through amber waves of grain. They plow through rocky soil up the sides of mountains behind strong horses or astride small, study tractors. Their harvest, though modest by midwestern standards, is hard-won.

In fact, our hardscrabble agriculture helped to make us more Blue than Gray during the Civil War. Unlike planters further south, farmers in the Big South Fork region couldn't grow cotton (the soil was too rocky), and so they didn't need slaves. We became fiercely loyal to the Union, sending more troops to serve in the Grand Army of the Republic than with the Confederacy. Indeed, when Tennessee finally seceded from the Union (the last to go and the first to return), Scott County seceded from Tennessee and briefly became the Independent State of Scott. The world little noted nor long remembered these passionate politics. On most maps of the era, the area was referred to as the "the wilderness."

The coal mines that once dotted the Big South Fork region yielded their treasures even more grudgingly than the soil. At Blue Heron, less poetically known as Mine 18, a few hundred men and boys (some as young as thirteen) braved danger, dust, and darkness to extract fifty-five carloads (2,800 tons) of coal every day, six days a week, from 1938 to 1962, for the Stearns Coal and Lumber Company.

▲ *A slow-running stream reflects the autumn sun.*

Grim as the daily routine could be, whimsy showed up in unexpected places. Miners had names like Willie ("Duck") Lyons, Norman ("Toots") Taylor, Raymond ("Monk") Strunk, and Earl ("Peanut") Shepherd. There were also lots of Ledbetters, but none of them had a nickname.

Blue Heron had several company-owned houses, which rented for $10 to $60 a month. One family moved seven times without leaving Blue Heron, trading up to larger (but never large) quarters, indoor plumbing, and other accoutrements of the upwardly mobile miner. A community bathhouse was built by the Stearns Company to settle a two-day strike, but the miners had to pay for the construction out of their wages. A company store was the commercial center of the community, purveying everything from eggs to eczema treatments. It was about the only place that would redeem company script—the private currency of the Stearns Coal and Lumber Company—in which many miners' wages were paid. When Tennessee Ernie Ford sang "I owe my soul to the company store," the people of Blue Heron knew too well what he meant.

I worked in a coal mine the summer after I returned from my service with the U.S. Navy at the end of World War II. My father thought it would be a good experience for me, and I was briefly in the employ of the Red Jacket Coal Company on Brimstone Creek.

My job was to set spads (place markers) to help survey the "rooms" in which miners would dig for coal. The rooms were never more than about forty inches tall. Miners would spend twelve hours a day on their knees, or standing with hunched-over backs, swinging pickaxes and swallowing dust. When they came out of the mines, they couldn't stand straight for a while. Ray Damron, the man for whom I worked, taught me how to roll on and roll off a conveyor belt to get around in the mine. Before the days of conveyor belts, mules were taken into the mines to cart the coal out, and boys were paid 54 cents a day to open and close the doors for the blindfolded mules.

With all the hardship, there were good times as well. The church was the social center of the mining community and the hotbed of young love. Social life consisted of frequent pie suppers and the reading aloud of Nancy Drew novels. There were contests for the prettiest girl and the ugliest girl, and young men vied for the attention of young ladies through the auctioning of pies that the young ladies had baked. Dancing was frowned upon, but other musical activity was encouraged. The Blue Heron Quartet was quite famous in its day and was in demand to sing at funerals all over Wayne and McCreary counties.

For all the loneliness of life in the "holler" and for all the danger that miners accepted as a way of life, there was a common sense that important work was being done at Blue Heron. As the mine was about to be closed for good, one miner recalled, "By '62, it was just obvious that we'd run the string out. It was heartbreaking. It was a job that I liked. The use of this coal in the nation had a meaning."

Up the road from Blue Heron was the larger community of Stearns, built by Justus Stearns of the Stearns Coal and Lumber Company. It is still there. The Stearns Hotel—torn down a few years ago—had what I, as a boy, considered the greatest dining room in the world.

On the southern fringe of the Big South Fork National River and Recreation Area is the community of Rugby, which, as the name suggests, is a bit of Britain transplanted to the Cumberlands. To be precise, Rugby is more Victorian than any town in England, frozen in time and happy about it.

Rugby was founded in 1880 by the aristocratic socialist Sir Thomas Hughes, author of *Tom Brown's School Days,* the forerunner of McGuffey's Readers. The town was a social experiment, intended as a New World haven for second and third sons of the British aristocracy, who by the laws of primogeniture could not inherit their fathers' property back home. These younger brothers, therefore, were sent to

▲ *Large tracts of pasture still dot the Big South Fork landscape.*

America to manage the more exotic family assets on the Cumberland Plateau. Under the tutelage of Sir Thomas, these proper English gentlemen built fifty-six Victorian homes, the Tabard Inn, Christ Church Episcopal, a bowling green, and the Hughes Library, which to this day houses no

volume published in the twentieth century.

These second sons of England took an idiosyncratic view of commerce. Their first business decision was to grow tomatoes, but rather than worry with the problems of cultivation, they formed a committee to design a label for their produce. They settled upon the image of a hand holding a large tomato, with the price stated in shillings and pence.

With this colorful exception, though, people in the Big South Fork area have been extraordinarily close to nature through the generations, including our own. Our livelihood has depended, by turns, on the fur trade, salt manufacture, oil for pharmaceutical uses, family farms, niter mining, logging, coal mining, moonshining, and harvesting herbal plants for tea and wild indigo for dyes.

THE MANAGEMENT

Fortunately, the National Park Service, which manages the Big South Fork National River and Recreation Area, is sensitive to this longtime love affair between the people and the land. Because this special unit of the national park system is brand new, the Park Service is determined to manage this area in a way that responds to the needs and desires of all kinds of people, while protecting and preserving the diversity of natural and cultural resources. The Big South Fork is a wilderness area from the blufflines down, which means, in the parlance of the Park Service, "no vehicles, comforts, or conveniences."

But on the plateau, the Park Service must foster peaceful coexistence among four-wheel-drive vehicles, bikers, horses, hikers, hunters, fishing enthusiasts, and even trappers. The bicyclists love Big South Fork, which *Bicycling* magazine has called the "mountain bike mecca of the East." This isn't easy. Horses, for some reason, don't like bicycles. Naturalists who come to look at the brilliant colors of the Big South Fork must share the park with hunters looking for deer.

Physically challenged nature lovers can get down to the wilderness area along the river without much difficulty, and so far everybody seems to enjoy the experience of the Big South Fork—whatever experience they're looking for.

So successful is the management of the park that people from all over the world are coming to see how it's done. A delegation from Thailand, where river-oriented parks are popular, recently visited the Big South Fork to see how so many constituencies can be served simultaneously.

THE MAKING OF A NATIONAL RIVER AND RECREATION AREA

And speaking of constituencies, I can't resist reciting a little of the political history of the Big South Fork National River and Recreation Area.

I am a distant cousin of the late Senator John Sherman Cooper of Kentucky, who as a young man cut timber in the Big South Fork area and who in 1920 surveyed much of it for the Southern Railway's railhead connecting Pulaski County, Kentucky, with Scott County, Tennessee.

In the late 1920s, plans were first drawn to develop this remarkable area. The Tennessee Electric Power Company (TEPCO) proposed to build a dam at Helenwood, where the New River and Clear Fork met, to produce hydroelectric power.

Because of the Depression, nothing came of that proposal, and TEPCO sold out in the 1930s to the newly created Tennessee Valley Authority (TVA). TVA was also interested in building a dam on the Big South Fork, at Devil's Jump, and Senator Cooper, Congressman Albert Gore, Sr., and my father, Howard H. Baker, Sr., tried for

▲ *Pines line the bluff of the East Rim Overlook.*

years to get congressional approval to have the U.S. Army Corps of Engineers construct this dam.

They secured the endorsements of the Eisenhower, Kennedy, and Johnson administrations. Five times the U.S. Senate voted to fund the project—in the Public Works Bills of 1962, 1963, 1965, 1966, and 1968—but each time the House of Representatives refused to give its consent.

By the time I arrived in Washington as a newly elected senator in 1967, this Devil's Jump dam project had been kicking around in one form or another for more than thirty years. I sort of inherited this issue from my father and for years afterward had no better luck than he had had getting final approval for a dam on the Big South Fork.

Finally, in the early 1970s, I suggested that we stop pushing for a dam and try to establish a national park in the area instead. I was advised by Bailey Guard, the very able and resourceful minority counsel to the Senate Environment and Public Works Committee (of which I was a member), that the Interior Committee had jurisdiction over national parks. I was further advised, politely but pointedly, that I had absolutely no influence on the Interior Committee.

Well, I said, what if our public works committee were to authorize the Corps of Engineers to build a Big South Fork national park and then turn it over to the Interior Department once it was finished?

The Corps of Engineers, advised Mr. Guard, did not build national parks. He was right. Even today, in the entire history of the corps, it has built only one national park area. You're reading about it now.

The Environment and Public Works Committee also authorizes road construction, and instead of a winding, treacherous road up the Cumberlands, we now have a modern, safe, easily navigable highway to the Big South Fork. In the words of lifelong Scott Countain Dr. Milford Thompson, "now any damn fool can get up here."

We look forward to seeing you.

▲ *Virginia white-tailed deer graze the once-farmed fields.*

Photographers are lured to the plateau region by its multitude ▶
of spring wildflowers.

▲ Lichens such as reindeer moss can be found beneath the conifers near Station Camp.

There are more than one dozen different species of trillium to be found during spring and summer. ▶

▲ *Dirt roads give evidence to the heavy logging the area once experienced.*

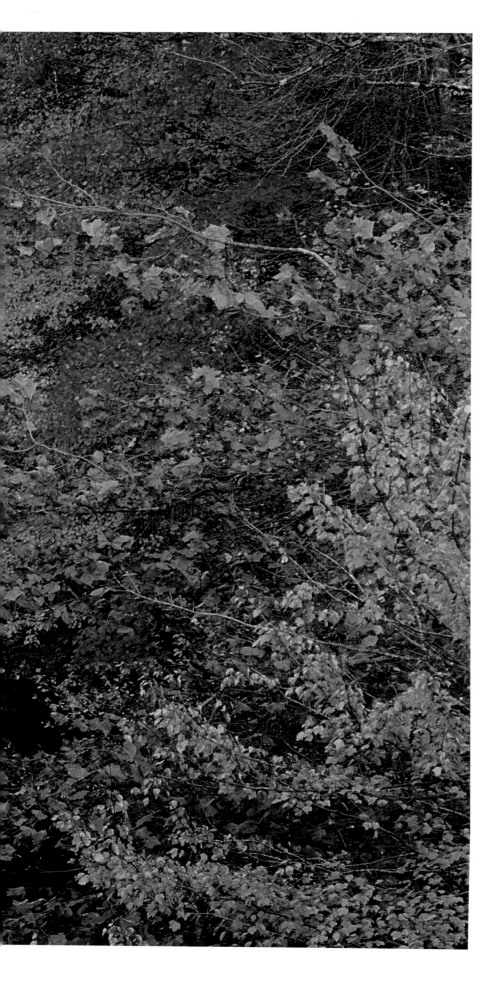

◄ *Autumn colors reflect in New River.*

Scrip

by Dr. Frank Thomas

Frank Thomas was born in the company town of Stearns, Kentucky, and, after serving in both the army and navy in World War II, reopened the dentistry practice of his late father. In 1959, he became vice president of the Stearns Coal & Lumber Company and in 1962, its president.

SCRIP was basically a cash advance paid to employees. No one was paid in scrip if he did not request it. There is a misconception that miners were paid in scrip at all times. The truth is that checks, convertible immediately into cash, were issued the first and fifteenth of each month. But if an employee was due, say, $100 on the fifteenth and needed $25 before then, he would be given $25 in paper scrip or metal tokens early and $75 on payday.

The scrip issued by the Stearns Coal and Lumber Company was probably different from that issued by smaller mines. Stearns operated in four or five counties and had several retail outlets. Most merchants in the area were willing to accept this scrip as payment because Stearns was sound financially. You could purchase anything from a casket to an automobile with scrip from Stearns. You could pay rent or utilities with this scrip. An uncle and cousin of mine were physicians in Oneida, and they, as well as my father who practiced dentistry in Stearns, gladly accepted scrip. If you wanted to convert scrip to cash, it usually meant selling it at a discount of 3 percent to 10 percent. Abuses, chiefly high prices at the company store, came in with scrip from smaller mines with only one store and no merchants that would accept it.

The timekeeper at a mine would post credit to an employee's account and issue scrip. A man would go to work in the morning and his wife would come in and say, "I want $10 in scrip." Some women, almost before their men would get underground, were at the window drawing scrip. The system caused many people to live from hand to mouth. On the other hand, probably 25 percent of the Stearns's employees never drew a penny in scrip and

another 20 percent drew it just on rare occasions.

Scrip was still used when I became associated with Stearns in 1959. We were convinced the system had outlived its usefulness, but getting rid of it was not easy. Merchants protested they would be forced to open credit accounts for customers. Many employees had been dependent on it and even drew scrip to pay their debts. Once an employee asked me to overrule a timekeeper who would not issue him scrip; he insisted he had to have it in order to make a car payment. We tried to ease the pain of withdrawing scrip by giving cash advances in limited amounts and by paying people weekly rather than twice a month.

By 1964, scrip was gone. But then there arrived credit cards with interest rates of 18 to 21 percent. People love debt and there is always a way to accommodate them.

You can still get scrip today. A full set of scrip—$5, $1, 50¢, a quarter, a dime, a nickel, and a penny—was worth $6.91 when issued; now a set is worth around $200 at flea markets and in antique stores.

▲ *Pine Creek flows into the Big South Fork River near the O & W Bridge.*

▲ *Bear Creek Overlook offers the only layered mountain view of Big South Fork. This is because elevations on both sides of the plateau are virtually the same.*

An orb web spider waits for the morning sun to evaporate drops of dew. ▶

▲ *Crimson maple leaves drop to a moss-carpeted forest floor.*

◄ *The 300-foot face of Indian Rock is a favorite wall for climbers.*

Yahoo Falls plummets over the ▶
edge of a large rock shelter,
allowing visitors to walk behind
the waterfall.

Water lilies cover one of the ▶▶
many ponds in the park. Late in
the evening, frogs use the floating
leaves as courtship platforms.

Rafters and kayakers ride the Big South Fork River, experiencing rapids that range from Class I to Class V.

◀ *Barns constructed of logs are still prevalent around Scott County.*

▲ *Fog is not uncommon along the plateau in the early morning hours.*

Sam Story runs the Bandy Creek Stables, which offers boarding for horses ▶
and guided horseback rides.

The March with General Jackson

by Kennedy Reed

Kennedy Reed served in Europe in World War II with the Army Air Corps and worked for the Tibbals Flooring Company, from which he retired as manager of the Shipping Department. Fond of the outdoors, he spends most of his time hunting, fishing, and gardening.

THE MEN in the Reed family have fought in every war, except for the Spanish-American War. We skipped that one. My great-grandfather Alan Reed supposedly marched from Scott County to Clinton, Tennessee. From Clinton, he marched to New Orleans, which is a little over 600 miles, to fight with General Andrew Jackson. I was figuring if you walked 25 miles a day, you got a long journey out there, twenty-four days or so. Can you imagine walking 600 miles just to shoot somebody?

Actually, the battle was fought after the war had ended. The War Department tried to discharge the soldiers in New Orleans after the war was over, and Jackson wouldn't do it. He deliberately disobeyed orders. He contended that his order was to march into New Orleans and to discharge the soldiers in Nashville. Nobody ever did anything to Jackson about that.

My great-grandfather was given a land grant to pay for part of his service. He applied for a pension many years later and was awarded a pension of $8 a month.

Of course, with the land grant you can't pinpoint it, whether this spot or this spot. He had three or four land grants, one dated 1805, one 1812, and one dated 1820 something. Most of them are small amounts, like maybe twenty-five acres at a time, or something along that line.

▲ *The moon sets over the Cumberland Plateau. Big South Fork is but a small section of the Appalachian Plateau, which stretches from southern New York to central Alabama.*

▲ *The Mine 18 tipple is a part of the Blue Heron exhibit, which interprets the area's early days of coal mining.*

◄ *Overlooking Lake Cumberland, the trailhead leads hikers to Yahoo Falls.*

Park researcher Steve Bakaletz holds a Big South Fork ▶ *crayfish. It is thought that all crayfish originated in the plateau region after the glaciers retreated.*

Making sorghum molasses has been a tradition of the members of the Reed family for years. They fuel the process with natural gas, a by-product of one of their oil wells.

Catching Moonshiners

by Jack Laxton

Scott County sheriff Jack Laxton was an elementary school classmate of Howard Baker. An avid horseman, he organized the Scott County Mounted Sheriff's Patrol and, with his deputies, rides throughout the Big South Fork National River and Recreation Area.

DURING the 1960s when I was sheriff of Scott County, I kept up with the number of moonshine stills that I was able to capture. The number was fifty-six. In most parts of the county there was probably one or two here and there. They were in Smoky, Brimstone, Jellico Creek, and one or two down along the brickyard. But this one particular time, along with Sheriff Jones from Fentress County, one of his deputies, and one of mine, we captured three at one time and some people with it. One fellow was coming from the still that they had been using. The other two were asleep. A copperhead was about fifteen to twenty feet from one of them that was asleep. One of the deputies shot that snake and, of course, they woke up. They were real surprised to see the law and, of course, they didn't want to see us. One of the deputies made the statement, "Hey, we just saved your life." The moonshiner said, "Hey, I'd rather have been bitten by that snake than have you fellows catch me."

You had to use a four-wheel drive to get into No Business on the Big South Fork. That was sort of a hot bed of moonshining. I got acquainted with one fellow, an old-timer that used to live down there. His name was Dewey Sweet; he's not with us any more. But he was telling me, "Hey, I was right on top of a cliff and was down there that day you got those three stills and had those fellows with you." He said, "I could have reached down and just about taken your hat off your head." He said, "You almost got mine." So, we didn't get them all; we missed one or two.

When the moonshiners put the stills together, they sometimes used just pure old mud—you know, the clay that they could wrap around there and that got pretty thick once it got dry. The really best stills were, of course, made of copper. They didn't use tin solder with them because that changed the taste. Then they daubed them with mud, and sometimes they stuffed them with corn silks or things like that.

We found one still down in the 1960s. We were out looking for a person that was lost. We had a lot of people out trying to find him. This person was sort of a mental hysterical person and he got lost, I guess. I believe Dorsey Rosser was with us. We got out of Scott County before we got the rescue squad organized, and we found a big moonshine still down there. We wasn't sure if it was Morgan County or Scott County, but Dorsey just laughed about that. He said, "Well, this will probably be the last one I'll ever have anything to do with."

Rockshelters were used. The moonshiners could be there and be dry, you know. And when they found a place like that, they were fortunate. They had a home within a home. They could sleep under that rock and work at the same time.

▲ Rock shelters provided a shield against the elements and home to the prehistoric Indians 10,000 to 800 years ago. Smoke deposits cover the ceilings, giving evidence to the use of cooking fires.

▲ *Amphibians are abundant throughout the park. This gray tree frog prepares to sing in order to attract a mate.*

◀ *Vultures ride thermals spiraling skyward, before plunging into the deep gorges.*

Mushrooms can be found beneath the ozone-resistant white pine at almost ▶
any time of the year.

▲ *Horseback riding is a favorite activity for many visitors. Riding clubs hold annual outings and competitions in the area.*

◄ *Banjo pickin' is part of the entertainment on the Big South Fork Scenic Railway.*

CAB. I

▲ *Fishing is a favorite sport in the Big South Fork.*

Chimney Rock stands against the sky like a giant monolith. Consisting of sandstone, these formations are quite fragile.

A yucca stands in contrast to the Blevins's barn near Bandy Creek. ▶

Spring rains turn small creeks into major tributaries. ▼

▲ *Summer wildflowers surround a pond near the General Slaven homestead.*

▲ *Twin Arches is one of the most popular geologic features of the park. South Arch has a span of more than 135 feet, while North Arch has a 93-foot span.*

▲ *The sun can be watched from atop a hill at the old King place as it sets over Bear Creek.*

◀ *One of the horses stabled at Bandy Creek peers out of her stall.*

A Crow Called Bill

by Neil Sexton

Neil Sexton, a lifelong resident of Scott County, has been employed by the Baker family for more than forty years. He is equally skilled at growing plants and fixing whatever needs repair. He roams the hills and hollows of the Big South Fork area hunting coons.

BILL wasn't a crow; that bird was a human being. Hell, it would squirrel hunt with me. It would go run the squirrels out. But it would never ride the Jeep, it would just fly over the top of it. And Bill went to school with the kids. He'd get out there every morning and sit on the tree and holler, "Bus, bus," for them kids. Well, he'd follow the bus to school and stay all day and fly back over across that bus with them kids.

Bill would sit on the windshield, but you couldn't get him inside. By God, he wouldn't ride inside. Crows love squirrel guts. You'd kill a squirrel and that's what Bill wanted; that's what he was waiting on. You'd kill the squirrel and he'd eat the damn guts. He'd call the dogs, and he's had my wife about to get whooped a dozen times for cussing and hollering at the neighbors when they thought it was her hollering at them.

He hated curly hair. There was a little boy that lived below us down there that had curly hair. Every time that kid would go up the road Bill would hit him right on the back of the head on that curly hair.

I started to work one morning, and he was always out there with me. You couldn't work on the automobiles—he'd carry the tools off. Anything that was bright, he'd fly off with it. Well, that morning I'd had the car started, you know, and the door open. All at once I heard the damn thing quit. I looked, and old Bill had them keys. I came a-running at him, and he took right down through that thicket. I never did see them keys no more. But when he died, we climbed up the oak tree in the yard there. I thought Bill was building a nest to lay eggs or something, but we climbed up there and in that nest he had Kathy's necklaces, money, and everything else he'd stolen somewhere. I don't know where he'd got it all.

Bill was a thief. I would never have another crow. You get attached to it like that. But I got that crow when he wasn't that big. He didn't have his eyes open or anything. And do you know what I fed it? Canned dog food. He'd open his mouth, you know, and I'd drop a little of that dog food in his mouth like a mother bird would. He broke his leg three times. He roosted on the garage door, and I didn't notice it. I'd go down there after work and not notice him, open that door up and shut it back and his leg would catch on there and break and I'd say, "Well, its gone." In two or three days, that damn leg would be back and he'd be healed. He was a pet and a half, ole Buster Bill.

▲ *Lake Elizabeth, situated between Huntsville and Oneida, plays host to early morning fishermen.*

▲ *A luna moth rests in the conifers, waiting to take wing as the night approaches.*

▲ *Daisies line the old logging roads. Lumbering was once a major industry in Big South Fork.*

▲ *Boy Scouts participate in the Order of the Arrow ceremony held at the Bandy Creek Visitor Center.*

A father and son fish near the Alum Ford boat ramp on the waters of ▶
Lake Cumberland.

▲ *A spider takes advantage of a cable support on the Burnt Mill Bridge.*

Autumn leaves create a mosaic of color near Leatherwood Ford.

▲ *A view of O & W Overlook reveals the O & W Bridge, which was closed for repairs and is once more open to automobile traffic.*

◄ *Songbirds like the tufted titmouse live in the mixed hardwood forests of the park.*

The First Commercial Oil Well

by Dr. Frank Thomas

THE OLDEST COMMERCIAL oil well in America is usually thought to be Drake's Well in Pennsylvania, which was drilled by people looking for oil. However, nearly fifty years earlier, in 1818, an oil well was drilled on land later owned by the Stearns Coal & Lumber Company and acquired in 1979 by the U.S. Park Service. The people drilling this well were looking for salt water.

In the early history of Kentucky, land grants were made for many reasons. Most people are familiar with grants made to Revolutionary War veterans. A thousand-acre grant on the Big South Fork was made to John Francis and Richard Slaven in 1818 on the condition that they produce 1,000 bushels of salt. This was done because salt was scarce in the area.

These two men contracted with three others to develop a salt works near the river, optimistically calling their site Saltville. After some complicated business deals, a well was started using a spring-driven rig. A bit that is supposed to have been a part of it is in the Stearns Museum. At a depth of more than 200 feet, a black substance, which they called "devil's tar," flowed from the well. Their attempt to produce salt had failed.

Martin Beatty, later a member of Congress, tried to make the best of the situation by constructing rafts to transport some of the oil to Nashville. When these wrecked, he arranged to take it there by oxen, where it was sold for medicinal purposes.

This is well documented. The Frankfort *Harvest* in 1819 had an article about the well. A letter from Marcus Huling, the man in charge of drilling the well, is in the Filson Museum. In it, Huling reveals their disappointment in the outcome of the well. He also mentions that some of the oil was sold in "Urop" (Europe). It was this evidence that led to the conclusion that this was a commercial well.

There are stories about the well overflowing, an early example of pollution of the beautiful Big South Fork. The local women were angry because their ducks were covered with oil.

There was a lawyer in Monticello named Tuttle who was very interested in this well and wrote a detailed account of it in the nineteenth century. In 1952, Kentucky's chief geologist did extensive research on it. At that time the site was cleaned up and restored to look as it had in 1818.

The geologist found an affidavit from a man whose father was present when the well was drilled. He retold his father's account of drilling the well using the spring drill, but he did not add anything new. But I was fascinated by his description of his father's death. The man was eleven when his father called him and his older brother to his bedside. "I'm dying," he said. "Son, when you die, you die from your feet up. My feet are getting cold and it's moving up on me. It's already moving up to my chest, and so I don't have long. I want to give you boys some advice. Always mind your mother and don't take apples out of other people's orchards."

▲ *From the river, visitors can sense the sculpting power of water as they gaze
up at the sheer bluffs.*

▲ *Visitors to Rugby can see firsthand the old printing presses used in the community's paper-printing business.*

◀ *Christ Church Episcopal is still used as a house of worship by residents of Rugby.*

Visitors to Rugby are greeted on special occasions by volunteers dressed in period costumes. ▶

A Rugby volunteer mixes the nineteenth and twentieth ▲
centuries as she photographs visitors in the historic area.

The old Ruby stove stands like a sentinel at the entrance to ▶
the Rugby print shop.

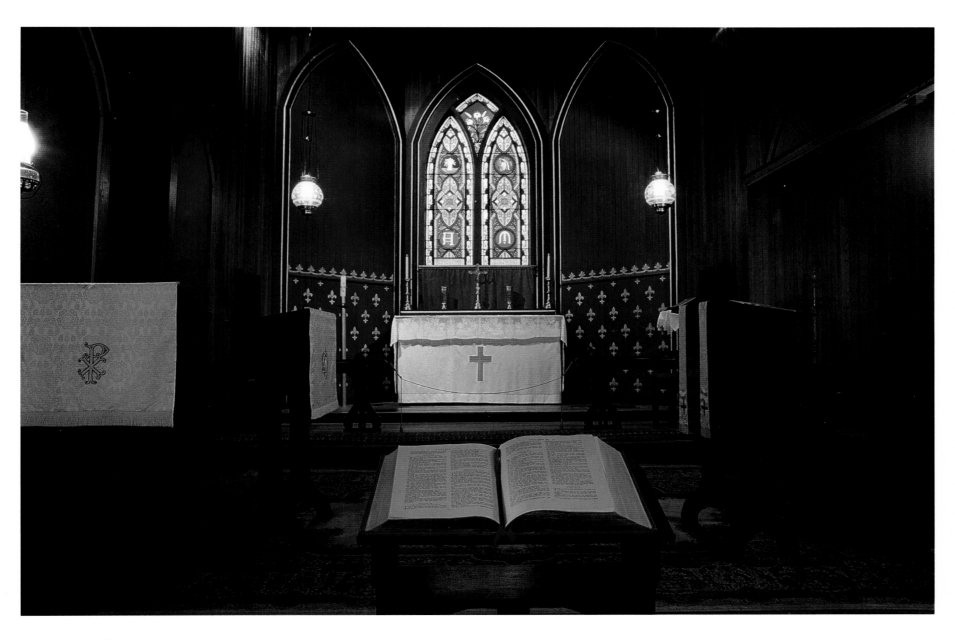

▲ *With hand-carved black walnut altar furniture and a dark pine interior,*
Christ Church Episcopal is considered the jewel of Rugby.

The flaking bark of ▶
the sycamore tree
creates abstract
patterns for park
visitors.

Standing near Maude's Crack, park visitors can see the sheer bluffs used by black vultures as nesting sites.

Late evening light separates the trees from the forest. ▶

New River Light

by Neil Sexton

I'VE SEEN THE DAMN THING. I don't know what it is. And nobody else knows what it is. It will light up till you can see forever, and it moves. It will go up and down, and it will just move around and then move off.

It happens back in the mountains. It's even been down in this field below my house. It runs after my boy, scared that boy plum to death. He said it was chasing him; it's never got him, but it's come awful close to it.

It's just a bluish bright light and it will change, you know. It will be a different color. It looks like the damn thing may be turning. You can't see through it; it's just like looking at a sealed beam headlight. It will get on top of like that mountain right there, just follow up, and it may turn down that hill, and come right down into the road. Not a bit of noise, no wind. I had it to go right across the hood of my damn Jeep many times.

The light is round; it changes shapes too. It will go down and it will raise back up, go down and it will raise back up, and it will get almost on the ground sometimes. I've seen it way up in the sky, but then it would come on down.

Other people have seen it—all of my boys, my daughter, and Raymond. Everybody's seen it. I don't know what the hell it is, but it's over there.

It's not always in the same place. I saw it plum down on what we call Jeffers Ridge, and I saw it over in different hollers, and saw it down in this big field, Rolins Field. It's been down in there.

I've watched the light for thirty minutes at a time. We got after it one night, or it got after us, whichever way you want to put it. We was coon hunting out of season. We turned down this big ridge, you know, and there was this big damn light. I told that boy of mine—Junior was with

me that night—that it was the game warden. He said, "I believe it is." We had a gun with us. I says, "Let's throw that gun out there and hide it." We did, and we eased on down. The light still kept moving, so I stopped. I said, "You walk on down there, see who it is, and holler back." He got on down there and well, hell, there wasn't nothing down there. It just moved on over the hill. It was that light. That was out on Jeffers Ridge.

It's there, and 500 people have seen it, I guess. Everybody's talked about it. Where it comes from, where it goes to, I don't know. Now, Jerry Willard and Johnnie Jeffers told this tale. They were down one of those hollers on Brimstone one night, and they said they looked and saw a light coming up the holler. They said it was making noise. There was three of them. The light whipped on by them and went up the holler a little piece and turned and came right back down again. I never saw that, but that's what Johnnie Jeffers and them told me.

I've seen it in the early morning and in the early part of the night and I've seen it at 12 or 1 o'clock at night. You never know when you're going to see it or where you're going to see it at. I'm so damn used to it, I don't pay attention to it any more. But one night, it came right across my Jeep and it lit that whole damn Jeep. You could see everything outside, everything. It just looked like you'd turned on a big light. It will be bluish looking and bright and then dimmer. I'd like to get a picture of it.

The light doesn't scare me a bit. I've stood and watched it come out right over the hill right down to three feet, come up over the other side of the hill or it might turn right up the holler. Sometimes your hair may sort of stand up a little. But a lot of people, they're scared of that thing.

▲ *The yellow-stained rocks of Oak Creek serve as a reminder that Big South Fork was once heavily mined for coal.*

▲ *The Burnt Mill area is a favorite launch spot for canoeists looking for a short ride on the river.*

Ferns cover the forest floor in the Honey Creek Pocket Wilderness ▶

◀ *Bird houses provide nesting cavities for songbirds like the eastern bluebird.*

▼ *"The mother lode" is what J. T. Baker calls this group of more than 100 beautiful yellow lady's-slippers.*

▲ *Scouting camporees are held annually at the Bandy Creek Visitor Complex.*

▲ *The evening sky is aglow with color as the sun sets over the plateau.*

◀ *Deep in the gorges of Big South Fork, new waterfalls are still being discovered like Joy Falls in Duncan hollow.*

Ginseng

by Kennedy Reed

I RAISED GINSENG. If you do it accordingly as you should, it is worth about $30 to $40 a pound. If you dig the wild ginseng up in the mountains, it's worth $250. But then the tamer, which is what we call what you cultivate, will produce possibly enough to equal it out because you know what you got. Possibly 99 percent of what ginseng is raised or dug in this country, so to speak, goes to China or Korea or somewhere. They won't let them raise it in China. Now in Korea, they have some I understand. I was looking in an old agricultural book just the other day—I believe it was from 1913, I'm not sure on that date—where the United States exported about a little over 200,000 pounds to China in 1913. I can remember when Howard Baker's uncle bought it, you know. That's a big thing in this country, digging ginseng. What you do is you dig it in the mountains where it grows, take the root off of it, bring it in, and dry it. You get it good and dry, then you sell it. Some merchants will buy it green, but they cut the price down 'cause it's going to dry out on them. They like the smaller roots better than they do the large ones. If you get a big one, it's so expensive nobody can buy it unless they break it up or grind it up or whatever, and so they prefer it to be smaller.

I got into it a few years ago, and I did it as a hobby, really. But then it got out of hand and got to be work. I had over 100,000 plants growing. Oh, it was ridiculous.

The best way to do it is to gather the seed. Now in the woods, of course, the seed falls off and comes back up in the wild. But the best way to do it if you're fooling with it is to gather those seeds in the fall of the year. See, the seed doesn't come up the next year. It takes two springs, the sec-

ond year for the seed to come up. You take those seeds and you put them in a box or something with a little sand in there. You put a layer of seed and a layer of sand and a layer of seed and a layer of sand, and you leave them in there for three or four weeks and the pulp comes off. Then when that pulp comes off, you take them out and dry them off and then you water test them. Then you do the same thing again. You put those seeds back in sand and so forth and so on, and then you go out there in the backyard somewhere and you dig a big hole in the ground and bury the box. You leave it there for a year till the next fall. Then you pick them up and plant them, and the next spring they'll come up. Now, if you let them fall off, where you're raising in your beds so to speak, they won't come up and the weeds will come up and if you're not careful the weeds will outdo the ginseng. Then you plant them, and you keep the weeds out. Boy, I'll tell you what, you get those roots as big as your arm. It's tremendous what you get.

There's an outfit that comes here from somewhere now, they set up at Co-op and up at Helenwood Foods, and buy it. Well, I still get out and dig it a little. I don't go into it too much, but I dig some.

Nobody uses ginseng here, not in this county that I know of. Of course, it is a growing fad in this country because quite a few athletes use it—baseball and football players, so forth and so on. The story is that there was some guy in China who lived to be 256 years old, outlived eighteen wives. He was a ginseng user.

Mrs. Terry and her grandson welcome campers stocking up on supplies at ▶
Terry & Terry's Grocery Store, on the eastern border of the park.

▲ *Nestled in a valley, Charit Creek Lodge hosts overnight hikers and horseback riders.*

▲ *Two young boys skip rocks across the river at Leatherwood Ford.*

▲ *The surface of the Big South Fork River is broken by scattered boulders.*

◀ *Violets carpet the forest floor in early spring.*

▼ *The red eft, juvenile stage of the red-spotted newt, is common along the Angel Falls Trail.*

▲ *With more than 130 miles of trails, Big South Fork is becoming one of
Tennessee's most popular horseback-riding areas.*

A turk's cap lily, still moist with morning dew, attracts amateur botanists ▶
to Leatherwood.

A view of Devil's Jump on one of many scenic overlooks reveals the ▶
treacherous turns loggers once had to negotiate.

Dentistry

by Dr. Frank Thomas

MY FATHER had been McCreary County's only dentist for many years. From the time he died in 1946 until I was released by the navy a few months later, there was no dentist in the county.

Establishing a practice back then was not difficult; the big problem was getting rest. Thirty-five years ago, when I left dental practice, you were expected to be on call twenty-four hours a day. There was always somebody wanting you to work on them because they had some sort of an emergency. The one thing my children remember about my practice is people coming by the house at night and on holidays and my going to the office with them. One Christmas Eve, when our twin daughters were less than two months old, I went to the office four times during the night to relieve pain. Between trips to the office and helping with the babies, I was exhausted. The next morning—just after my fourth trip to the office—I went to a friend who was leaving town for Christmas and asked if I could sleep in his house.

Nothing in the world made my wife madder than someone honking outside to call me to the door. If the phone rang, it didn't upset her even if it awakened us. But someone honking infuriated her. Last Saturday, we went to pick up some friends and Mary suggested I honk to let them know we were there. "Oh, no," I said. "They're not going to talk about me the way you used to talk about honkers."

Mitchell Thomas, my father, was a graduate of Vanderbilt and the first dentist here. Stearns was a new town and unusual for this part of the country. There was electrical service, water, and telephones in the homes. That was rare in small towns in Kentucky and Tennessee then. My mother, who was a thirteen-year-old girl in Huntsville when Stearns was founded in 1902, heard tales of rich men from Michigan building new towns, new mills, and a railroad. Most important, these people paid everyone on time and in full.

My father came to Stearns and stayed a couple of years, but he wasn't getting the amount of dental practice he wanted. He was considering leaving when R. L. Stearns urged him to stay. The company allowed him to pick the site he wanted and built a new home for him, a home my mother lived in for fifty-seven years. The rent for that eight-room house was $21 per month; the rent for the office was $7.50 per month, including heat and water.

A dentist was expected to make house calls on occasion. My first visit to a mining camp was when I tagged along with my father. I remember seeing rooms papered with old newspapers to keep cold air from seeping through the cracks in the walls.

My most humorous house call was to attend to a man well over eighty who was bedfast. My uncle, who was a physician, went along to check the old man's heart. After doing what I thought was a pain-free extraction, the man relaxed and told us about his past dental experiences. He had worked on a steamship that traveled from Burnside to Nashville and he had visited several dentists along the river. He described in vivid detail their skills or lack thereof. Finally, he looked at me and stated that of all the dentists he had seen, one outshone them all. I puffed up and asked the obvious question, "Who was he?"

My uncle never forgot the answer: "There was a blacksmith who lived about a mile from here. He was the best tooth puller I ever seed."

The park's ponds are frequented by large herds of deer in the early morning and late afternoon hours. ▶

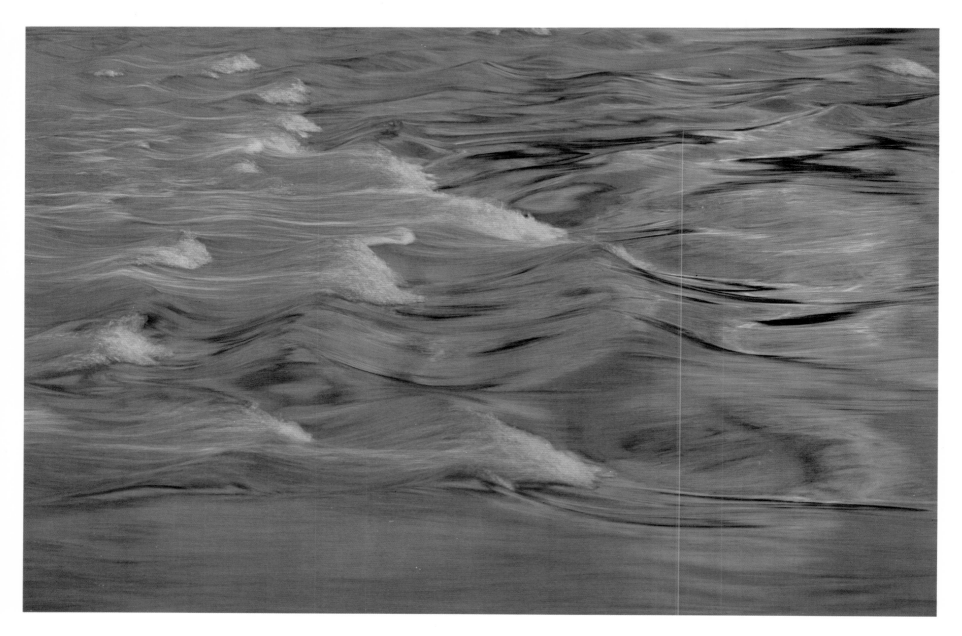

▲ *Fall colors reflect in the rapids near Burnt Mill Bridge.*

Blackberry thickets cover fence lines once used on the old farmsteads. ▶

▲ *Fog enshrouds a field of goldenrods near Bear Creek Overlook.*

▲ *Perhaps the most widely recognized view of the park is from the Leatherwood Ford Bridge.*

◀ *Spring wildflowers like the celandine poppy carpet the forest floor. There are more than 1,000 different species of flowers within the park's boundaries.*

▲ *Shooting stars line the plateau rim.*

◀ *Virginia bluebells grow along the banks of the Big South Fork.*

▲ *Snow blankets the New River Gorge.*

The Mother Lode

by J. T. Baker

James Toomey Baker was born in Huntsville and developed an interest in lady's-slippers when his mother took him and his sister on "wildflower tours." He worked in Michigan and California and returned to Tennessee where he worked for a water company and took up wildflower studies again.

L ORD, I can't even remember what year this was. But somewhere in the dim distant past, not all that far back really, but a number of years ago, I got word somehow, I can't remember who told me or how I found out, that the Tennessee Native Plant Society was fixing to have a field trip going up around Rugby to observe the Cumberland rosemary, which is an endangered plant that's up in this territory. I had always been kind of curious about the Cumberland rosemary and decided that I would go over and see if they'd take me to where I could observe it also. So I went over to Rugby the day that the Native Plant Society was going to be there and I took some wildflower photographs with me.

So I went over there and I found the Native Plant Society—the main ones that I found were Tom Patrick and Dennis Horn. Do you know Trillium Tom? Well, he was over at U.T. back in the old days. I think he's moved on to some other college or university now. But he's a botanist whose specialty is trillium. And then Dennis Horn—I guess you might call him a lay botanist who works down at Tullahoma. Dennis is a very knowledgeable guy. He probably knows about botany, but that's not his profession.

But anyway, I told them, I said, my hobby is photographing flowers and here's my credentials. And I spread out a whole bunch of 8 x 10 color prints on the table over at the Harrow Road Cafe. And they were looking at some of these, and I had this one identified as *Cypripedium calceolus*, variety pubescens, which has a common name of large yellow lady's-slipper. Either Dennis or Tom, one, said, "You know, this looks like it might be that lady's-slipper that Max Medley is doing some work on." (Max Medley is a botanist up in Kentucky.)

They indicated that they would like to go see this plant, and I told them, "Well, the photograph was taken in a fellow's yard where he had transplanted it, see." And so they decided they'd like to go see it. We went over to Paul Phillips's, which is where I'd taken the picture, so they could observe the plant. When they saw them, they all decided they'd like to see them in the wild. So we commenced to go down to the river so we could look at them in the wild.

I'm going to have to back up just a little bit because before all this happened, a year or two before this, I had asked Freeman Walker to take me out in the woods and show me some yellow lady's-slippers, which he did. He took me down somewhere near the mouth of the Lick Branch. So when we left Paul's, we all went down to where these lady's-slippers had been dug up, you know, in the wild. We got down there and it was down near the river, about the first bench up from the river.

Anyway, I was thinking I might go see if I could find any Cumberland rosemary around New River near Huntsville. So about the next day or the following day, Monday or Tuesday, I went down to the river, just below Huntsville, down to what used to be called the Town Ford, but nobody fords it hardly any more. I couldn't find any Cumberland rosemary. So I just started walking back toward my vehicle. On my way there, I kind of looked up the creek and I thought, there's a likely looking place for wildflowers. I just headed up the creek. Cain Creek is the name of the creek. I hadn't gone ten steps when suddenly I saw this yellow lady's-slipper. It didn't have a bloom on it, but it was a *Kentuskyense,* which is what they finally named that species. I've got my reflexes conditioned for the foliage of yellow lady's-slippers, for all lady's-slippers. Anyway, I found that this yellow lady's-slipper was not blooming, but there was no doubt what kind it was, you know.

While I was standing there looking at it, the light went on, like it does in the funny papers. I had an idea. I started thinking, now here I am, here is this yellow lady's-slipper. I have now seen it in the wild three or four places and each one of these places has been, you know, a similar habitat. It's almost identical—all near the river, about the first bench up from the river, near the mouth of a creek or branch. And so I thought—well, this is where deductive reasoning came in—I thought the chances are I could go to similar places up and down the river and maybe find some more. Well, I got out the TVA map and looked for similar situations. The first one I went to was the Mother Lode.

Of course, I found other colonies of yellow lady's-slippers since then, but nothing ever compared to the Mother Lode that I found. So there you have it.

▲ *A local mountain bike club takes advantage of one of the many bike trails in the park.*

◄ *Lichens cover large boulders and the forest floor near Station Camp.*

▲ *Heavy fog rising from the gorge enshrouds ridges near the East Rim Overlook.*

▲ *Fall leaves seem to be suspended as they float on the water surface.*

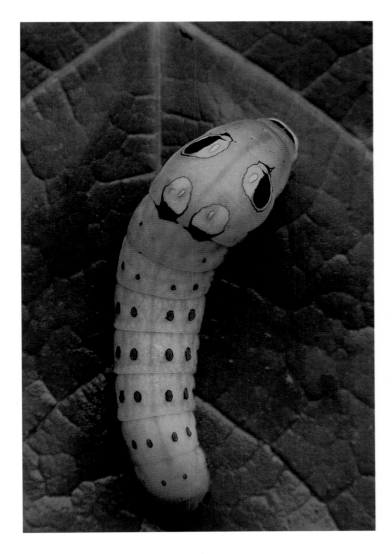

▲ *A caterpillar searches for a meal before its transformation into a butterfly.*

◀ *A pileated woodpecker pauses after excavating its nesting cavity.*

During the summer months, ferns are abundant in ▶ *the region around Station Camp.*

The Baker Church

by Howard H. Baker, Jr.

Huntsville has three churches, two Baptist and one Presbyterian. The story goes that there was a tourist coming through town one Sunday morning who stopped at the Texaco station and said, "Pardon me, but could you tell me where in Huntsville is Christ's Church?" And the fellow says, "Let me think. Now the Byrds' got a church, and the Rectors' got a church. Baker's got a church, but I don't believe Christ's got a church in this town."

I belong to the Presbyterian Church, which is sort of known as the Baker Church. It has been going there for generations, but it's a little church, and as a little church it suffers the indignity of new preachers right out of seminary. Especially during the Vietnam War they were just terrible. They were all wild hairs and radicals; some of them I think were almost bolsheviks. Anyway, one particular preacher was a young fellow who was trying to acquaint the congregation with his position and views and was talking about how the church has changed, entered the modern era, and has different attitudes toward public affairs, drinking, and sex. And Lloyd Scates, who was in his eighties and an elder stood up and said, "Preacher, all I can say about that is that if the church has changed its attitude on sex, it's a dirty trick on an old man."

Lloyd Scates, elder in the Huntsville Presbyterian Church. ▶

▲ *Young men fish the river near Station Camp.*

◀ *Petals drop from bloodroot, one of the early spring bloomers.*

The setting sun reflects off the Big South Fork River, which flows through Bear Creek Gorge.